WE HAVE COME TO BELIEVE

COUNTRY VALLEY PRESS

We have come to believe

Charlie Mehrhoff

Copyright ©2020 Charlie Mehrhoff
Cover photos by Nora Mehrhoff

ISBN 978-0-9820196-6-5
Printed in the United States of America

Country Valley Press
1308 W. Washington St.
Carson City, NV 89703

countryvalley.wordpress.com
countryvalley@mac.com

for

Deon Rehemah

– poetess –

my friend in Luoland

CONTENTS

Foreword by Clint Frakes	ix
That snap in the air...	1
Only the Unknown is vast enough...	2
The night wind...	3
Crucible:	4
We have come to believe...	5
How small and lifeless	6
That the wheel become so large...	7
Time was from the breast of...	8
Humanity never...	9
Poetry, true poetry...	10
Haunted:	11
Were it not for doubt...	12
That voice inside your head...	13
Here...	14
Just a few friends talking politics...	15
On Dereliction of Cult Behavior:	16
If a thought is not connected...	17
God without religion.	18
Presence:	19
What wears you down to nothing?	20
Broken rules.	21
Where the mind goes...	22

From the empty cup...	23
East:	24
What is still worth something...	25
Death Poem:	26
I beg no coffin between my bones...	27
Fading, the cry...	28
Oh heron! Above...	29
Physicists and astronomers...	30
Clear, so clear...	31
The idol maker attempts to pour...	32
Turn off the moonlight.	33
If only we praised the Great Spirit...	34
How to have the Word of God...	35
A man from the city driving...	36
Men who never had to work the land...	37
The bigot who was nourished...	38
Now conjure for this planet...	39
The door to the forest...	40
Homage	41
The Sky at Night	42

FOREWORD

American poetry desperately needs the work that follows: a corrective to the language of poetic messaging and a soulful interrogation of our intentions with it. Yet the correction is less stern than suggestive. To praise Mehrhoff simply as a master minimalist is to miss the point. His poetic conscience entails minimalism in its understanding of the literary needs of our time. While his poems have aphoristic value, they far transcend that medium. One recalls Pound's definition of the function of image: *to render an emotional complexity in an instant.* He is a borderless poet that has aligned with no tribe, equally comfortable in the misty mountain shrines of Han Shan as in the flume of smoke of Hells Angels riders. To mistake these lean units of verse as literary simplicity is equally to miss his message. Mehrhoff is a poet of complexity willing to explore the minute banalities of his inherited culture within the frame of broad Taoist horizons and the sacred texts of the masters. He implores us to re-embrace the ancient necessities of language as fuel for human evolution. His hard-earned distillation of the poetic moment is the seasoned refinement of consummate human-heartedness, flavored by devoted study of the esoteric and boots-on-the-ground citizenship. The imperative: that the opposing poles of the human condition be embraced by the language of spiritual affirmation.

There is valuable instruction in these poems. Mehrhoff has kicked his spade into the earth in hope of redeeming the primary service of language and poetry: to instruct the soul. Corollary to that, he gently scolds us for desecrating language in our collective neglect to rarify our words as medicine for human survival. Mehrhoff aptly models a poetic alternative to the apathy and self-absorption that plagues American culture. There is an artistic patience in his work that allows for inevitable truth-telling—both with nuance and urgency. His work is a commentary on the relationship between spiritual existence and language itself, and how they create and reflect each other. He challenges us to measure the words that we use versus the properties and principles they are meant to signify:

> How small and lifeless Love
> were it merely
> the opposite of hate.

An emotionally cogent poet will often supply the yardstick by which we might read her or him, and help us co-create a culture within the contract of poet/reader. Mehrhoff is that poet, and he instills a high directive as to where poetry might be aimed:

> Poetry, true poetry
> to spark a riot of forgiveness
> and unconditional love.
>
> The rest is whining,
> Mere insolence
>
> An affront to the essence
> of the Word

Yet, he is not hesitant to express his frustration in how language is sacrificed for anything less than the pursuit of true revelation:

> Just a few friends talking politics,
> yet my ears are already filled with shit.
>
> I put on the tea water and pray for another stroke
> of loneliness.

These poems are many-layered in their leanness, containers of cultural, historic and philosophical balance, not just "short poems." They have no expiration date. Mehrhoff is a truth-seeker without being a moralist and insists that we collect these shards on our own terms to ponder our responsibility in how they apply. Each poem is a mirror of human universals underscored by the baseline of ephemerality and the hardest-earned truths of human navigation. Mehrhoff's spiritual instruction expresses as a refined lens, a vehicle of interpretation—and the mechanism of recognition:

> If a thought is not connected to spreading love
> in this world
> that thought comes from Below...

> That voice inside your head
> that keeps telling you to pray.
>
> Bow down with it.

> ...if when you finally arrive there, at your long sought-after peace and solitude, if you are still there, being able to sense your own presence, you have not gone far enough.

This American poet has located the currency of "message" via image, and elegantly refuses to sacrifice one for the other. The balance therein is the soul of poetry. His philosophy arrives without sacrificing the image; on the contrary, it serves in the delicate placement of image—but never gratuitously. One feels the tracks of fasting Taoist mountain monks through urban alleys within a single phrase. These poems hold the grand ineffable in graceful counterpoint to the irony of quotidian phenomena, all while celebrating the curiosity of our fragmented condition. Yet, the exigencies of his subjects are precise and located with humor and astute observation. While the shape and length of these poems seem to mimic classical contemplative forms, they are quite different in embracing post-modern complexities and cultural/historic backstory.

The test of the poet truly representative of his generation (and fit for the next) is often seen as much in what he resists as in what he embraces. Mehrhoff refuses topical opportunism, "woke" platitudes and moral superiority. You will find no artifice in these poems, yet there is high art. There is humor without the interference of personality; there is statement without doctrine; and there is urgency without hyperbole. He stays true to the Objectivist foundations so evident in his lineage to resist the romantic in favor of the virtue of clean sight, and gives evidence of his wisdom without forcing conclusions:

> That the wheel become so large
> that it no longer need roll
> to get
> from here to there.
>
> How love must grow
> throughout this world.

Mehrhoff's work treasures the tension between human divinity and human frailty as an imperative in its own right. This tension is the soul of his literary contribution. The immortal is framed with the transient—the empirical by the mythological—and these are the primary polarities of humanity itself. If one thing is clear about this poet's ethos, it is that the poem holds the contour of revelation. Allow these poems to serve as the "harmonic topography" that charts the soul's long journey to recognition.

Clint Frakes
8.15.20

For the man who understands, no sacrifice exists only purification.

-Carlos Saurés

That snap in the air,
some other poet
has broken the language.

Only the Unknown is vast enough
to embrace this flood of pilgrims.

Welcome!

The night wind,
fierce,
tore our shelter to Heaven.

Crucible:

For what we believe forgive us.
We have been impersonating mortals for so long
that we have forgotten who we were
to begin with.

Time to rise up and dust the poverty from these rags.

Take my hand. We will walk along the edge and listen
to the infrastructure creak and groan.

We will listen for the echo of the Unknown.

Only the Unknown is without limits.
And perception is death.

Nothing has changed.
Constantly.

Within reach stands all that is reaching.

Bright glowing ancestral bone.

Young gods running wild in some nascent universe.

Running out into the fresh chill of some spring morning
to listen to the robins sing

a few notes
between the sorrow and the bliss.

We have come to believe
that when there are no people left to converse
or to read in a given language,
that when there is no one left to understand
or to make use of a language
then that language is dead.

If the above holds true then that language
was never alive in the first place.

A living language creates its own realm,
even its own universe,
for souls to lift
their voices throughout.

A living language
being
its own voice.

How small and lifeless
Love

were it merely
the opposite of Hate.

That the wheel become so large
that it no longer need roll
to get
from there to there.

How love must grow
throughout this world.

Time was from the breast of the amoeba, from placenta dangling across sweetgrass, wild raspberry, clover.

Time was we thirsted upon what rain that pooled within each other's flesh. There was no lack of celestial reflections, myriad nuclei, to orbit our loving house, to purple her earthen floors towards honey at twilight.

Time was we saw no vine swift enough to choke the robin's egg, and the space between twins as the magic air to bathe in. We knew each day to possess its own definition of luxury. The first day: in streams of quicksilver. The second day: alongside albino quadrupeds. The third: with camels bearing snow. The fourth: through open doors in the stratosphere, ushered by cherubim. We made love in regions unchartered. Dizzy, lost within our mating dance, closing our eyes to Orion, waking up with faces full of dew. Focusing upon a mantra not yet of this world. Watching fairies painting moonbeams, actual moonbeams. Seeing the traveler becoming pollen. Listening for the first bird to sing, and to be there to call it *song*.

We became the stone worn into oblivion by the kisses of pilgrims. We became the comet skipping like a runaway child across the ink of unreachable space. We filled buckets from the river, carrying a drink of her rhythm back.

All tables swollen. Nourishment coaxed from vines. Granitic clusters laced with twig-meal, edges where lichen did curl. All seeds enchanted with the Unknown, tracks of the gazelle sprouting from it.

Humanity never
hated itself
all this much.

We have just forgotten
where
and how
to reach

for those
words of love,
leaving us

stranded here
amid this language
of violence.

O poet!
You have your work.

Poetry, true poetry
to spark a riot of forgiveness
and unconditional love.

The rest is whining
mere insolence,

an affront to the essence
of the Word.

Haunted:

Have you ever made a promise
that you could not keep?

Peace,
shelter
and food

for all of the children.

Were it not for doubt
there would not be this vast hole in my faith,
vast enough for God
to strut on through.

That voice inside your head
that keeps telling you to pray.

Bow down with it.

Here
we don't give out awards for books
except to say: this is true.

Our poets
return to the fields each morning.

And when the earth
comes to roll between the sun and the moon
we all
cast the shadow of eclipse.

Just a few friends talking politics,
yet my ears are already filled with shit.

I put on the tea water and pray for another stroke
of loneliness.

On Dereliction of Cult Behavior:

Has the ritual evolved to some higher,
to some other,
state?
Or has it become distorted?

From a mushroom covered stump
with candles in the wood
to a concrete altar surrounded with floodlights
and amplification.

Where could the essence possibly be
any less present?

A circular way to the first question:
in your quest for enlightenment
–throughout your journeys,
your meditations,
your wanderings
–if when you finally arrive there,
at your long sought-after peace and solitude,
if you are still there,
being able to sense your own presence,
you have not gone far enough.

Run from the concrete altar.
Set the stump aflame.

If a thought is not connected to spreading love
in this world
that thought comes from Below.

The mind is battleground.

Each negative thought must be cut away
the moment it attempts to blossom.

And the practice of love
will be refined to such a degree
as to become
the highest of all the art forms.

This is the destiny
of the *Whirling Sword.

       2017 Kenya

The Whirling Sword of Flame – since the fall of man, the sword, at the eastern boundary of the Garden of Eden, guards the way to the Tree of Life.

God without religion.
Freedom without chains.
Love without conditions.

Presence:

Years of walking
entranced
among the dappled,
dancing sunlight.
And years of listening
to the slow trickle of raindrops,
to the wind through leaves,
to hummingbirds
about their nests –

the whole forest sings
and singing,
when suddenly
we come to realize
that each and every
tree
is the Tree
of Life –

and with every branch
being
a perch

for the Almighty.

What wears you down to nothing?
What strips your shelter and skin away?
What breaks you down to a mere howl of wind
across the altar?

Yes!

Broken rules.
Broken hearts.
Broken promises.

Pieces for everybody.

Where the mind goes
when the emptiness comes to dwell
is not my concern,

as long as the emptiness comes
to dwell.

From the empty cup – the emptiness,
every drop of it.

East:

Free as an unknown god in skies unchartered.

Naked as a thought without a mind to grasp it.

Roaring asylum.

Harmonic topography of perfection.

Chimes sounding without the metal
ever having been
extracted from the ore.

The echo of celestial bliss
splashing from the horn.

As when the dawn
dawns upon itself.

What is still worth something to a dead man?
Ask yourself this.

Death Poem:

Let it be someone else's turn
to lay upon their back
all naked,
cold
and awestruck
with the clouds.

Enough for me.

I beg no coffin between my bones and this earth.
May the worm pass through as swiftly as a comet
across the night sky.

This life!

Fading, the cry
of some distant bird—

poet's gravestone.

Oh heron! Above
it all
so quickly.

Physicists and astronomers have long known
that the gravity emanated by a mass bends light.
This being so
proves the particle composition of light,
which leads some to wonder
if there exists a light so complete,
so dense, so overwhelming in its being
that no mass can hold sway over it.

This light we know
to be
the Way.

Clear,
so clear

that when one looks upon the Master
all that is seen is

the Way.

The idol maker attempts to pour the entire ocean into a wine glass.

Impossible business.

Turn off the moonlight.
Remove the sun and all radiant bodies from the heavens.
Shut down the power grids.
Outlaw electricity and every kind of manmade flame.

Yet this world will never orbit in complete and total darkness.

There will always be a few subatomic particles
scattered lonely and radiant.

Not even nuclear holocaust will wipe them out.

There are you saints.

If only we praised the Great Spirit
with the same fervor that we curse one another

the celestial abundance
would rain down from the night sky
and fill our cups with starshine.

How to have the Word of God
written upon your heart—

grow
a bigger heart.

A man from the city driving through farm country looks at his hands,

feels nothing but shame.

Men who never had to work the land.
There's your mob for you.

The bigot who was nourished
in the womb.

This thought
somehow
makes forgiveness easy.

Now conjure for this planet a guerrilla peace,
devastating acts of goodwill and loving-kindness.

Break out the engines of beauty.
Stand up inside yourself.

Pray for an outbreak of humanity
within humanity.

Carve a messiah
out of your bleaching bones.

The door to the forest
slams shut —

wild man
coming home.

Homage:

In 2016, a teacher at the Korando Center, Kenya handed me a poem entitled *The Sky at Night*. It was written by a young girl named Deon Rehemah.

For nearly half a century I had been in a fervent relationship with the Word, or so I thought.

Yet, it was not until reading Deon's poem that I found myself on my knees. *The Sky at Night* allowed me to feel it all. It was the poem I had been living for.

My prayer is that Deon continues to write, that Africa, that humanity, nurtures her great gift. If Deon stays the path this world will be in the very best of hands.

                                            c. mehrhoff
                                            6.17.20

THE SKY AT NIGHT

The sky at night is like a big city full of men and beasts.
But never once has anyone killed a fowl or a goat.
No lion has ever killed its prey.
There are no accidents.
Nothing is ever lost.
Everything knows its way.

                    Deon Rehemah

www.ingramcontent.com/pod-product-compliance
Lightning Source LLC
Chambersburg PA
CBHW022125040426
42450CB00006B/852